Dying Is Forbidden
In Longyearbyen
by
Katie Metcalfe

www.nordlandpublishing.com

Copyright

Dedication

To my parents

Contents

Acknowledgements

I would like to extend my thanks to Michael and Markus at Nordland Publishing, without whom this collection would not have been possible. Their patience and passion, commitment and drive always inspires and provides great motivation.

My grateful thanks also go out to Bob Beagrie, Andy Willoughby, Chris Stewart, Amir Darwish, Julie Edgell, Kev Howard, Clair Harbon, Andrea Storey, Cat Cooke, Sara Elisabeth Andersson, Becca Campbell and Stewart Jon Forth for their continued support and encouragement over the years.

Foreword

Since my childhood, I have felt an extraordinarily strong attachment to the north, with its forested, mountainous landscapes, winter and death, occultism and all sorts of unsettling subjects. I was the strange little girl in school, who always had a book of ghost stories hidden on her lap, while teachers talked about algebra, geometry and religion. I was the girl with the vivid imagination, who would hear long dead wolves singing mournful songs while out walking with friends over the desolate North Yorkshire Moors.

These early and continued fascinations have shaped the writing I create today. Through my creative work, I attempt to explore my attachments to shadows and the north, particularly Scandinavia - where my heart calls home.

The poems you will find in this collection explore the north from multiple perspectives. You will be taken back in time to 1349 where you will look through the eyes of a young girl whose home in the west fjords of Norway is being ravaged by the Black Death. You will experience what it is like to be attacked and buried alive by a brown bear. You will witness the closing hours of the life of a young man who believes the answer to his problems lies in the cold wilderness of the far north.

From Over The Mountains

Word comes over the mountains
of the Black Death moving
towards our farmstead.

A heavy melancholy falls over my
small family, like the waterlogged
cloak of a dead warrior.

My older sister begins to scream,
powerful, terrible wails that make
my hands and legs quiver, grow weak
as the slick limbs of a lamb newly born.

My mother falls to her knees, rocks, speaks
in tongues I've never heard, like the hermit
in the forest a day's journey from here.

The hermit who thinks every cloudberry
growing in Norway belongs to him.

My father remains quiet, breathing heavily,
bending to stock the fire, though we're only
partly through the day, the lefse from the
morning bake still cooling on the table.

There is little talking as the dark moves
through the forest to greet us.

With a final goodbye to my mother and sister,
Father does what he said he would when
we first caught news of the sweeping death.
I didn't believe him when he spoke then.
I thought families were supposed to live
and then die together.

The storehouse is cool. He shows me where
he has hidden oats, water and meat, lefse,
cheese and flatbread, enough for many months.

The hound is waiting outside the door. I hear
him snuffling at the gap, see his wet nose
prodding through.

I ask for him to stay. Father shakes his head.
I don't argue. I know the hound gives him hope.

There are red marks on my upper arm, from
where he pulled me from the farm
to the storehouse.

He sees me touching them, says 'I didn't want
to hold your hand a last time.'

He closes me in. An iron key turns in the lock.
He says he will leave it hanging outside on
a hook. His voice is thick with despair.
It sinks deep into my bones.
And I am alone.

I press my cheek against the closest wall
to where my family are. My father cuts
the throats of the cows and sheep.

Blood feeds the earth for hours.
I pray to our old Gods for mercy,
for the lives of my family.

I pray to the new God, until the words
become tangled with my tongue and
I can say no more.

Nights and days pass. I eat little. Sleep often.
Every morning I reach for the door.
It is always locked.

There were voices yesterday, slight, meek,
tight with pain. Today, the outside world is quiet.
I wonder if the plague took the birds too.

I shout until I taste blood. Weep until
my face adopts a thick crust of salt.
I sleep until I scream myself awake.

The routine resumes until my body and
head are as empty as my dead mother's hands.

In the night, I hear wolves emerge from the forest.
I peer through the small window, watch them
sniff the crumpled bodies of my loved ones.

They leave quietly with clean mouths.
I wonder what happened to the hound,
if my father drowned him in the river.
or if he held onto him as his body
blistered, popped and fell apart.

The world is tense. Waiting. I can feel it
even behind these four, wooden walls.
The smell of death makes my head ache,
until the first frost arrives and clears
the land of the stench of rot.

I have never wanted winter before now.
A group of survivors arrive five days
after my family fell.

They share what is left of my oats and bread,
tell me to grieve for the last time, then, to
wipe myself clean, before moving over
the mountains with them, for a new beginning
at the head of a different fjord.

The Hut

Silence has become
too precious here.

Tuning in with myself
is practically impossible.

The fire in my heart
has been asleep for months.

I want to seek a way
through unexplored forests,
and build a home.

Somewhere to breathe,
to wander off course.

Somewhere to make love
as snow howls and beats
against walls to be let in.

Somewhere to get frail
without hardly noticing.

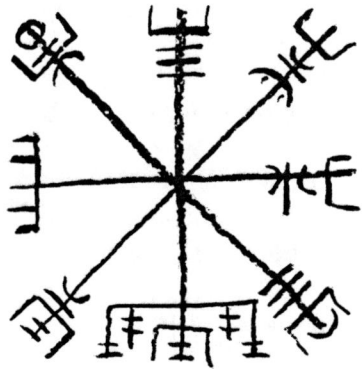

Of Sixteen Years

I watch you pawing a half moon
into the frost crusted earth.

It was winter the day your mother died,
the day we brought you into the house.

I remember the rusted blood around
the yawning wound on her belly.

I remember driving away the wolves,
their snouts gory with stinking entrails.

I remember your thin legs and small
hooves. The way you were curled
up behind your mother's body.

A week later and you were running
with the dogs through the spring grass.

Last night, the air in the house was tight.

I counted and re-counted the meat stocks
in the freezer, flipped through the cuts
smoking. I was hoping there would be
a forgotten stack of protein.

I want to let you see one last winter through.

But I know, deep down in a place where
my real feelings convulse, that it's going
to have to be now, before the snow.

Else you will be rotting in the early
spring sun and we will be hungry.
I can't do it though. I can't put the gun
behind your ear, make the shot that will

startle the mountains and bring you down.

I shake half a bag of oats onto the earth,
follow it with a handful of apricots, clotted
together. They were always your favourite.

It is my son's first kill and he is proud to take it,
I can tell by the way he walks towards you.

I turn, pretend to look into the distance,
where gigantic storm clouds are gathering.

But really, my eyes are screwed shut
and I am crying. I wipe my nose across
the foul sleeve of my overalls.

The fall of your body is loud.
Then there is silence and my son's
long fingers on my shoulder, squeezing
the taught muscles, stiff with misery.

'It is time dad,' he says.
'She won't feel anything now.'

And you lie as if sleeping.

A Night In October

It is October. Cold has started to stir
in air that was, just a week ago,
comfortable to breathe, to swallow.

The forest opposite my bedroom window,
where, a few days ago, I found a sheep
with its stomach pulled out, sings long,
mournful songs, as leaves start to take flight,
and old trees grow gaunt and bitter.

At night, the forest's songs grows longer,
more dismal and heart-breaking.

I sit on my bed, knees pulled up, watching
light be consumed by the dark shroud of the forest.

Wolves have been extinct in England
for hundreds of years, but tonight they
have returned. Tonight, they are moving
like spectres along paths I too follow.
Tonight they will feast on the remains
of that heavy sheep that wandered down
from the moors and lost its way.

I bite my knuckles. Downstairs, my dad
watches TV, lets the fire burn low. My mum
takes a load of washing off the hanging
drying rack, layers on another load.
The dog is drowsy on the sheepskin rug.

I want to go downstairs, ask from the door
if we can keep the fire burning until morning,
until we go to school.

But I don't. I stay in bed, my book
clutched between my legs. I stay upstairs
and watch the forest. I smell the wolves,
imagine their lips pulled back in snarling smiles
as they lope across paths I too follow.

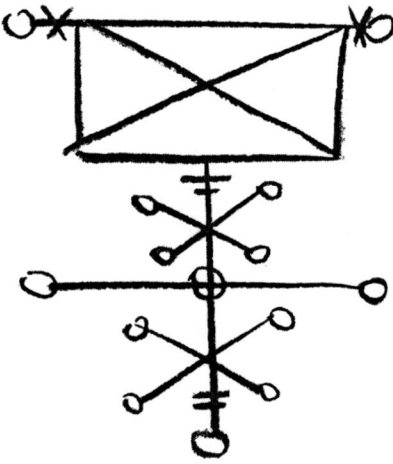

At The Stake

Our last meal together was broth made
thick with the meat from a fat rabbit.

You, bold as thunder, quiet as falling ash,
caught the grey field runner while the sun
threw fiery arrows across the tired land.

And here we stand, about to meet the fire.
Our punishment for living quietly, for pans
simmering with herbs, for burning candles
made with wolf fat and scented with honey.

They have bound you with the same thick rope
as I am bound with. Your small front legs
are tied up behind your head, as my arms are.

You stopped making noises a while ago.
The spiders and ants from the forest have fled
the severed limbs of the trees that stood
around our now ruined home.

I tell you that we will burn today and I know
you understand, because your swollen eyes
became still, and you stop trying to struggle
from the bindings cutting into your soft skin.

The owl has come to honour us. On the roof
of a market stall, selling hot cakes and cider,
he perches, the slim body of a ferret
threaded between his talons.

The horizon is ready to hand me a cloak,
and guide us both away from this violent end.

There is some oak among the kindling,
the smell of my woodland guardian is powerful

and comforting, like the smell of my father's
beard after a day foraging in the woods.

We hold eye contact, while flames flicker
towards us, hot and fast, and in your eyes I see
the morning I found you in a nest of brambling,
eyes barely open, mouth ripped open by a predator.

I stitched your skin with a thorn and sheep's wool,
and carried you home in my basket, under a soft
blanket of elderflowers, honeysuckle and heather.

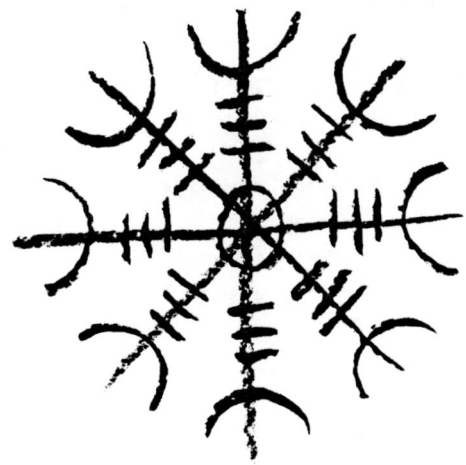

Old Age

My hair is frost white at the roots
and long. The tips brush the back
of my ankles when I move from
my desk to the window, to the garden,
to the trees that stretch for miles
with no break in-between for roads,
or houses or fields thick with corn.

You are still asleep, light hair
tossed across the pillows.

I pass the grizzly we have come
to know. He raises his face,
snout tinged blue from berries.

He recognises the way I tilt my head,
and goes back to snuffling in the bushes.

I pass the lake where we still swim naked.
Where we lay on our backs and float, holding
hands, talking about details we can see
in the sky, until we are floating in the milky
light of the moon, and get hungry
for bread and cheese and tea.

I pass the rocks where I posed naked
all those years ago, and you took shot
after careless shot with your camera.

You told me I was the most beautiful ghost
you had ever seen, and we made love there,
on the rocks, under the hot gaze of the sun.

I pause at the place where we buried
our daughter when winter took her for his own.
I move on, past the place where we brought

down the elk, and stroked his great head
as we ate his heart in thin slithers and silence.

I pass the clearing where we first heard
the wolves, and climbed trees to watch
the pack gather and run beneath us.

I stop, when I hear thunder boom,
when the air becomes hazy, and the rain
starts to thrash down hard and fast.

I stand, in a place I've never paused
before, next to a tree I've never smelt.
I lift my face to the sky and confess.

I haven't uttered the words I am afraid to die
since were both young and raw and grinning.

I will return to our home, I will smile
when we eat supper and light candles,
and kiss with mouths open. It will be
another month until my next confession.

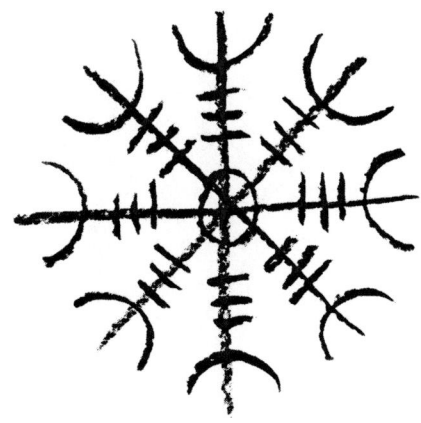

The Space Between Moments

When I wake, the silence is so utterly complete
that the sound of my own breath is too loud
and I crave a second heartbeat.

I hear my bones shift one way, then the other.
They are unsettled.

There are no familiar footprints in the snow.

When I outwit ice on the road, and manage
to stay upright, there is no one around to see.
I say 'nice one' to myself, 'you're getting good at this.' I
speak really, really quietly.

Before I left, you cradled my hands in yours.
I ran the tips of my fingers over the ridges
on your nails, and remembered how doing so
used to soothe me as a child at times of stress.

You told me how proud you were,
and how you wish you had said it more often.

It has been snowing for two days straight now,
and the space between moments stretches.

Utburd

The forest wants to give you a name,
and you are transfixed by the tops of the firs
and the stars. You reach out to touch them,
to touch all of what's above, but I wrap your arms
tight, and edge on through the snow in the dark,
away from the village, towards the mountains.

As I unwrap you from your blankets, I expect
a scream. Cold closed my mouth a long time ago.
But you are quiet. You look past me.

In the snow melt, they find your bones,
marked with the bite of the wolf.
I lower my head when the news comes,
and remember your silence.

I am scared to look over my shoulder
while I split logs at dusk, for I have seen you
outdoors, when the sun has set beneath the fjord.
I have heard you crying, seen you moving
out from between the shadows of the trees.

From inside, behind the window, I watch you
pulling your tiny body forward, disappearing
only when the sun burns up the dew.

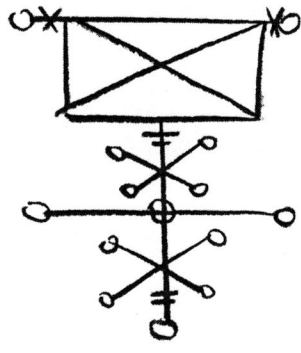

Deep Trauma

Your body has suffered deep trauma,
and they're not sure you're going
to wake up from this clot of sleep.

I hold your little finger, the way I did
when we were kids, and you would say,
'hold my hand so the wolves don't get us.'

I had convinced you there were wolves
on the moor, hidden in the heather, waiting.

I want the wolves to find the hospital,
pad along the fiery white corridors,
doctors thinking they're a beautiful hoax.
I want them to come here, to your room.

My heart has developed new ridges
and canyons over you. I can't remember
the last time it felt smooth.

Before the crash, before I saw you
destroyed by fog and a hot burst
of difficult conversation, I told you
it was time to drop the depression,
time to sweat through the withdrawal.

You told me you weren't ready,
that it wasn't time.

I rolled my eyes, turned away
while you fell backwards again
into the battlefield.

We have all agreed in the turning off
of your life support machine.

Quietly, you slip over, your features
more fragile than I've ever seen,
and tranquil.

In my fit of mid-afternoon dreams,
you are on the moor dancing barefoot,
and there are wolves with you.

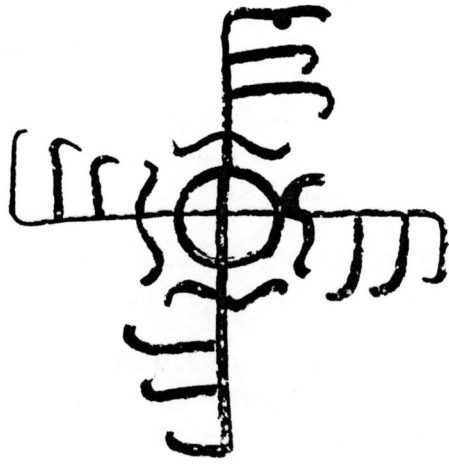

Lost

She had been chattering her teeth for hours,
twisting her fine hair into knots too complicated
for any parent to release.

That is what I wanted to tell the police.
I wanted to say we hadn't let our eyes off her
the entire time, that she was always a few skips ahead,
exemplifying the serenity of childhood.

I wanted to say that we had seen the end of autumn
and the beginning of winter with her fingers around ours.

The trees are the only ones speaking.
They creak and sigh in their own language.
They have nothing to say to me.

I remember the pattern of her pulse, but not
the exact part of the path where we lost her.

The search continues through the afternoon,
and past dusk. A new frost hardens the snow,
makes the overgrowth sparkle, the ground
splinter and crack like old bones.

I stumble, head thick with aftershock,
heart closed up tight with shame.

In my head, I imagine that she has made it
to the forest's border, where farmed fields
touch the chaos of the forest. Where wolves
turn around and lope back the way they'd come.

I imagine that a farmer picked her up, has her
wrapped in sheepskin and drinking milk
that's been warmed in a pan.

I overhear one of the volunteers whisper
how beautiful and peaceful the white dark
of the forest is, how a little girl with cotton socks
and blonde hair would settle right in, like she
was a part of it from the very beginning.

Pale Desert

The tracks I made yesterday are gone,
lost under the weight of new snowfall,
never to be seen by a human eye again.

I stand and study the pale land,
honest as salt, powerful as the moon.

The new fall looks like the remnants
of stars that have exploded and scattered.

A few miles away, snow is protecting crops
from the cold. A few more miles away,
a wolf is lying above ground, belly full.

The world is as calm as the feathers
on the back of a sleeping goose.

I take off, making fresh tracks, bringing
my knees up high. I run like I did when
I was a child, when I needed to touch
every bit of winter before it disappeared.

On the smooth white sands, great patches
of ice rest, shimmering like liquid moonstone.

The fresh snow under the trees
absorbs all sound. I'm quiet as I move,
as though I'm walking across furs.

Where the ground is exposed, it wears
a pale, shell delicate crown.
My feet break through, the air fills
with the noise of splintering.

I could stay out here all day, watching
snow shift with the wind, but my ears
are thick with cold, my cheeks starting
to blister. It is time to hurry home, to
cradle tea and thaw.

Twenty Five Minutes From Home

The Inuit say that if it is cold enough,
words will freeze in the air, and not reach
the ears of those who need to hear them,
until the spring melt.

I hope the Inuit are right. There is so much
I want you and your Dad to know.

I wound down the window, then panicked
in case I shouted into the dark for too long,
and it would refuse to budge back up again.

The last question you asked me was if polar bears
would survive a move to Antarctica. I said if they did
they would demolish the penguin population.

I expected you to flinch at this, but you didn't.
You nodded, and said 'good job nobody has tried it then.'

It is ironic that just hours ago, we were watching
the snow fall after turning off all the lights
and electrical appliances in the house.

I was as excited as you were.

The carton of semi-skimmed milk has started
to turn into slush. I shake it. It sounds like
river ice breaking up.

I can just hear myself breathe.
Clouds gather around my mouth.
I didn't know until now, how quietly
snow can consume everything.

Quiet Love

You observe the flight of migrating birds,
study the movement and shape of clouds.

You know the moon and her halos,
are fluent with the depth of the thaw.

With a handful of snow, you smothered
our deformed first born, and I still
chew your boots each morning.

In arguments, you drag me out
onto the ice and we fight, then love
each other quietly under furs.

I wonder if you would love me more
if I didn't flinch when the wolf howled?

We breathe quickly, sigh when
the moment is ready, while
the warm cluster of family sleep.

The pain of coming in to see you
lying with another is like coughing up
pieces of my ruined heart.

I walk away, pulling my spirit
behind me, like a seal recently
hauled dead from the ocean.

A Country Lane In Yorkshire

This is the country lane I used
to walk with my granddad.

His hand could always close
completely over mine.
It was almost magic.

I dodge the same yawning potholes,
filled with quivering black water.

Once, the water was clear,
cluttered with bundles
of frogspawn.

We brought some home once,
dropped it gently into the garden pond,
watched the black specks grow.

There is a photograph of my dad
as a young boy. He's standing here
where I stand now.

The photo is in sepia and has
a coffee stain in the top right corner,
near the heads of his two brothers.

They are looking directly into the eye
of the camera, all mushroom haircuts
and chalky smiles.

My dad is looking shyly
at his hobnail boots, hands deep
in his pockets, hair nearly in his eyes.

In the photo, my dad is wearing
a parka with a map pocket at the front.

There is a compass around his neck,
though he knows the back woods
as well as the rhythm of his own pulse

For a moment, I consider pushing
my way through a gap in the hedge
bordering the lane from the woods.

It takes everything in my power not
to try and see if my granddad is waiting
on the other side.

I continue on, come to the boundary
of Studley Deer Park. The gate is locked.
I turn around and slowly start back.

The sun is deep beneath the branches
of bent oaks where witches once
grappled, choked and swung.

The air is starting to get cold
and foxes bark in the woods.

At home, nanna will be mashing tea.
Granddad will still be gone.

The Vanishing Village of Angikuni

I work to fight the cold curdling
my blood to slush. The Arctic night
pushes hard upon my shoulders. It wants
me to take all of its weight for a while.

Fatigue eats from my feet up, but I don't
have to worry much longer. Inuit are
good folk, they will feed me hot fish.

On the outskirts of the settlement,
62 degrees North, I shout a greeting
in direction of roughhewn huts.

But my own voice comes back
to meet me. My snowshoes loud
as trees felled into ice crusted drifts.

The absence of children's voices,
unsettles my heart, sends it to all
corners of my body, but not back
to its original place.

The full moon waits.
There is no smoke to meet it.

I hold hands with fear, stagger past
wave battered kayaks. I pull back
caribou skin flaps on one hut,
then another and another.

A scream moves at the back
of my throat, but only a whimper
escapes. I sound like my son
when he is still awake and hears
the wolves gather.

A pot of stewed caribou,
thick with mould. A child's
half mended sealskin coat, bone
needle imbedded, deserted mid-stitch.
There is no sign of a struggle.

In every hut, a single rifle leans
on the wall beside the door.

I revisit my flesh for the first time
in many hours, as I near the border
of the village. The iced burial ground
is open, graves are crevasses, only
I can see to the bottom and they are vacant.

I spot sled dog carcasses tied with
thick rope to scrubby trees.
I leave quickly, humming hymns.

The Mounties think I sing colourful songs
of the north, until they themselves smell
moulded caribou, spot loaded rifles,
find no footprints.

On Sea Ice

You understand now and for the first
time in your long life you whine.

I remember your opening breath.
The sun was but a pale spot in the sky.
You sucked your mother's milk
off my fingers.

The air is sour with the scent of weeping.
We will never venture south, over sea ice
for supplies, then come home again.

You started weak, but are now powerfully
built, with an imposing physique.

Loyalty, affection, intelligence
all run marrow deep, but they know
none of this, the mounted police.

To them, you're nothing but a risk,
allowing us to roam. They don't know
we use your urine for medicine.
They don't understand dogs equal life.

My children have to bury their puppies.

You were looking forward to the hunt today,
but now your sister miscarries while she dies.

Your brother trails blood over the hill
as second, third, fourth shots fail to kill.

The others have no way to return home.

On our hunts, I would shout *Nanuq*!
You all knew what I meant, and your lungs
competed with those of the raven.

You howl in pain. A bastard in red missed
your heart, but takes another suck
on a cigarette before he makes
you ready for the fire.

The smell will draw the bears.

The distance for furs and food
will be dangerous now, exhausting.

I take your fur as they light the first piece
of driftwood. I cradle your heavy heart
in two hands.

In my ears there will always
be the echo of your last howl.

I have nothing now.
I have nothing.

The line 'Echo of your last howl' was inspired by a film entitled
'Echo of the last howl' a documentary examining the slaughter of
Inuit sled dogs in the 1950's and 1960's.

The poem's last two lines are the words of Johnny Munick, an
Inuit who recalls the devastating event when his team of sled
dogs were executed right before embarking on a hunting trip.
They were already in their harnesses.

Greeting The Crossfire

The day you told me it was terminal,
the first snow was gathering in the sky.
I told you I loved you. That was all
I could manage, my brain wet paper heavy.

You sip your tea more slowly than before,
closing your eyes before swallowing.
This is a good cup. I know because
behind your scarf you're crying.

In a small voice, you talk about when
you would get books from the library,
start with the one that was least promising.
You say you wish you hadn't done that.

I try and avoid looking at the library returns
shelf when I pass it in the hall. It's packed
with guides to Canada, 24 tips for better sex,
recipe books for a Christmas you won't see.

You ask if this is God's idea of bloodsport,
and if the tumours killing you are his hounds.

You say you feel frustration in your ribs.
You want to crack them open, pull them out.
I think you would if you had the strength.

I want to bury you at night so I can
pretend it's not really happening.

But you want it first thing in the morning.
You have never really liked the dark.

We don't go on the Internet now.
You have deleted Facebook and all your
other social media accounts.

'I don't want to be there after I'm not'
you say, gathering jpegs of photos to go
on a hard drive you won't plug in again.

I offer to go to Boots, print some off,
buy a new album. You agree.

'I can take it with me,' you say,
before your voice fades into an
anticlimactic whisper. I can just
hear that faint fizz of your pulse.

You say you don't want to die.
Your words cut through the border
of my skin, sink into my bones.

All I can think about for weeks is how
darkness will deepen as soil wraps itself
around you, your one designer dress
and our bulging photo album.

When you become too weak to talk,
I hold your hands. You're about to greet
the crossfire. There will be howling
when you're gone.

Katie Metcalfe

Late Autumn Afternoon
In Rural England

You are the one who hears
the weak hum of a dying bee.
There is an honest apology as
you bring your heel down
on his tiny, furred body.

'How hard it must be to never
go home again,' you say.

Your heart is naked today.
And swollen.

We walk on. The sun as small
as the head of a pin.

We watch a weasel under thick
brambling suckle the bones
of a young rabbit.

His black eyes catch us.
He continues on, little teeth
flashing in the dying light.

From the wood behind an old,
dry stone wall, a fox screams.

The cold will come soon,
and with it the whispering dark.

Survival

You use moss to control the bleeding
on your shoulders and abdomen.

I prepared for the worst, when you
faced the bear and went down.

But you triumphed over what was
the last resort - the fight back.

It takes a while for you to find your feet.

I watch the body of the bear relax,
sink a little into the forest floor,
damp with blood and rain.

You skin the tongue.
We will keep it as meat for the journey.

The liquid in the bear's eyes makes
a strong glue when mixed with tree sap.

We create a container from its stomach lining,
make it taught with cold river water.

We leave the bear where he fell, tip our faces
towards the sky. The pole star will direct us home.

Whitby At Night

In the warren of the old town,
hunkered down behind the cliffs,
whitewashed cottages face outwards
towards the raging north sea.

The small harbour town of Whitby
is quickly quietening down after a hot
day of commotion.

I have walked these worn cobblestones
a thousand times or more, but never
this late and never alone.

It isn't long before the ancient port
is hushed and dark.

Seagulls have finished trawling the streets
for lost chips, and at the bottom
of The 199 Steps I stand and wait.

A couple come down, her knickers
clutched tightly in one hand, his fingers
wrapped around her waist.

They don't catch my eye and disappear.
I hear them start to run.

It is past the witching hour when
I catch the sound of claws moving
down across the steps of stone

I keep my eyes open and the moon disappears.

I remain motionless while the hound
circles me. Heavy, coarse fur
scratches my bare legs.

Its growl is deep and for the first time,
I am truly afraid.

Then hands, cold as corpse wax candles
are upon me and I know this is the end.

There is the sad cry of a curlew as I am
lifted up and above the frothing sea,
heavy wings beat the blackened sky.

The cobbles will lose their chill
in the pearly light of dawn.

Nets will be drawn in, stuffed
with gasping fish.

Tourists will ascend the steps
counting, pausing to rest when
their heart demands it.

He Came From The Town

He came from the town
with his heart in a wet knot.

'The North has all the answers,'
he says, looking me in the eye.

His fat shot of whisky is untouched.

Under the thick glass bottom
rest my initials, carved back when
my Grandfather first showed me
how to tap into the trees for syrup.

'You will want to get some grease
on those,' I say, tipping my glass
towards the patches scattered like
a spell of frost across the plateau
of his clean hands.

His white fingernails are all intact.

He shakes his head. I can taste
the hair products he used at the back
of my throat. Fruits I've never tasted before,
only read about in books.

'Her parts were open to anyone,' he says,
roughing up his hair. It falls back into place.

I can hear the anger growling in his veins,
even over the scream of the storm.

He stands, weak boots on his feet,
a coat with no hood on his back.
His whisky sits untouched opposite me.
'Tomorrow I will find a bear and bring it down,'

he says, flexing his wrecked hands. I watch
the skin crack like the crust of week old loaf.

The bar falls quiet. Everyone turns to look,
then return to their fingerprint patterned glasses.
The bar slowly rustles back into life,
as the town boy charges out into the cold.

I give him a few minutes, then follow,
his whisky shot warming my chest.

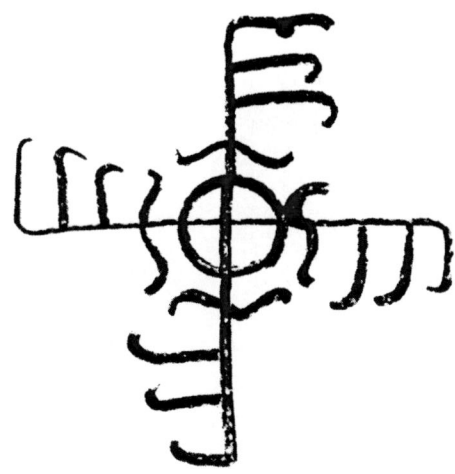

Witness

Your elbow is arrow sharp,
but I clutch you tighter,
squeezing an ebbing warmth
as your blood starts to cool,
pool and settle.

You wanted death to find you
here, where stars stuff the sky.

I remember the candle crackling
in the lantern, the night before
we left the safety of the cabin.

I remember the hot devastation
of our last fuck. How you gripped
my waist and moved to the rhythm
of my heartbeat.

Now loss pummels my torso
as your body decomposes.

I sit and watch the process.
I eat two nuts and four raisins
from the trail mix bag.

I take a sip of water.

I remember, four years ago today,
shouting through the glass of your
hospital window. I shouted 'I love you,'
my emotions a cradle of knots until
you said it back and managed a smile.

The wolves come after two days.
From the tree I watch them pull you
into pieces. They take out your throat,

tongue, heart, lungs, liver.
I never imagined I would ever see
these intimate parts of your being.

You would have wanted this.

The wolves don't look, but I know
they know I'm balancing on the sixth branch up.

They walk slowly away, bellies low.
You've made the ghosts
of the forest drowsy.

I wait until the ravens and the rain
have moved on, then scrabble through
your bones for things to keep.

I take a piece of your spine, an intact rib,
a bone from your middle finger.

I leave the ring I gave you, half-buried
in leaf mulch and new earth.

I sit with your bones for a while,
listen to the curious bees attracted
by the sweet smell of your remains.

I sleep, the taste of your beautiful wreckage
in my mouth.

When I wake, nature's little ones are
circling you, excited. It's time to leave.

I pack your bones in the face cloth we shared,
dry blood under my nails.

I follow the sun home.

The White One

The white whale is hauled ashore,
his heavy body leaving deep, blood
stained passages in damp shale.

I thank this slow swimmer for coming
to the coast, for not leaving when the rest
of his family made for the open sea.

As his body relaxes into the sand,
the ripped flesh around his open
wound flutters.

I think of how our organs
and skeletons are so similar.

I stand and watch my father
and grandfather cut into
our beached friend.

Blood, thick intestines
spill into the churning shallows.

The dogs bray for the meaty soup,
pulling themselves back on their hind legs,
their mouths all teeth and dripping gums.

This beluga is long, healthy and fat.
Plenty will come from his carcass.

Anticipation swings about our heads,
like bear hides drying in the brisk
north wind. We are all impatient to eat.

I crave the oily taste, its chewy texture,
the satisfaction that I have been fed
by the sea.

My father and grandfather work fast.
Their knives are sharp, the blades
slip soundlessly through the blubber,
until all that is left is a memory of a
white whale in blood diluted with sea water.

We stock the fire with meat, chew cubes
of blubber, while mother tells us how she
once put her head into ice cluttered water,
when her father was busy gutting a seal.

My mother tells us how she listened
to the white ones gather around the ice cap
and sing a song of celebration to their creator,
Sedna, mother of the Arctic deep.

Disappearing Ice

This is not our ice.
This is not our weather.

Our circle is contaminated.

Today we drink soot,
eat meat needled with toxins.

In my dreams, the ice is thick
again and clean.

This morning, we found the headless
body of a seal, drifting in the shallows.

My small son stuck his head
into the gaping wound.

'The insides are missing,'
he shouted. 'Hungry walruses
sucked them away,' I told him.

He came to me, wrapped his arms
around my neck. I kissed the stinking
skin on his forehead.

The drums, dances and stories
which held the ice together,
have fallen silent.

The waves are changing shape.

I can no longer draw a map from memory,
because the land changes faster
than I can blink.

At night the ocean screams.

We sit in our house at night listening,
afraid to fall asleep.

The Arctic is a battleground,
the aroma of oil and chemicals
makes my young ones ill.

I came face to face with a polar bear,
as the last light thumbed its way
across the land.

I could smell his rotting teeth.
He lay down before me and died.

I didn't take anything from him.
My knife would have brought
more poison to the surface

I left him there, rocking gently
on shifting ice, black water
licking at his nose.

Please Don't

Can I take back the bullet, please?
Replace the splinter of bone, cups of blood.
The piece of flesh and patch of fur?

She floundered in the snow before I shot,
looked over her shoulder.

Her eyes said, 'please don't.'

I thought about putting away my gun,
turning for home. But I wasn't brought up to do so.

I heard the wolves last night,
I heard the story of a long war on the wind.

We watch the white horizon, guns steady.
'He'll come back for his woman'
father says. 'They always do.'

He is right. A black nomad returns,
gives a quick, frantic bark. Ravens circle.
His presence pulls my heart out of its box.

I imagine the feeling in his belly, that ache
for his companion setting in like mountain stone.
He is not used to this, being on the other side of
victory.

The bullet touches neatly behind his ear
before I have time to find my breath.

The wind picks up, the ravens dip
to dance in the blood and I have no choice.

We cut the throats, so their souls
can escape to the skies and I wonder
about their naked firstborn.

Will it be grown?

The pack will sit with their dead
and tonight the moon will be silent.

Dying Is Forbidden
In Longyearbyen

'You should say goodbye to the children,'
the doctor tells me, his hand a damp weight
on top of mine.

'I will make arrangements for your flight home,'
he says, scribbling with a fountain pen on a page
dense with words, that blur in and out of focus.
The scratching pen irritates my ears.

I clench my teeth until I hear something crack
and crumble at the back of my mouth.

But what does it matter now?

I am a dying woman, sitting in an office
that smells like the forests I abandoned
for tundra and dangerous dances with
the north wind and pale kings.

It is forbidden to be a dying person in Longyearbyen.
It is forbidden to pass over to the other side here.
Nobody will bury your body in this town.

Seventy years ago, the cemetery closed its gates.
The permafrost disabled decomposition.
Here, 78 degrees north, the dead from
generations past lay as if asleep.

Home. Home is here.
Home is Longyearbyen.
Home is Svalbard.

Home is in this mountain valley.
Home is where I carry a gun
when going to buy groceries.

Gossip about my terminal condition
is loud in reception.

The topic of conversation shifts easily
to the Icefjord no longer freezing,
to the glaciers swiftly thinning.

The children are drawing yellow suns
with wax crayons for the windows
of the kindergarden.

They ask where I am going.
I tell them home.
They ask me when I will be
making pictures on the blackboard again.
I say I won't.

They find this confusing.
They ask when they will learn
how to shoot a bear. I tell them
sooner than they think.

I leave everything as it is.
My computer on standby, dishes
draining, damp clothes spread across
my two dining room table chairs.

I leave my wooden house
unlocked as always.
I learnt how to shoot a bear the evening
I arrived in Longyearbyen.

Tonight, I walk the polar bear's land
unarmed. I left my mittens in my rucksack.

It's common practise to throw them
in the snow to distract an aggressive
male or a protective sow.

Tomorrow, I am supposed to board a plane
to mainland Norway. I hope the snow
drifts over my prints.

I am naked underneath my parka
and the cold is astonishing.

My muscles shiver then stiffen.
I can feel the hair on my arms rise.
My eyelids are starting to freeze.

There is a dead silence in the dark ahead.
The cold brings me to my knees
when I can no longer see the
lights of town.

I pull back my parka, lie belly-down
on the snow. Everything has started to burn.

I hear the bear before I see him.
He has seen me. He is hungry.

The moon lights up the proud,
pale king, movingly steadily towards me.
We lock eyes, before his long face grows
hazy, and I feel my head thickening with sleep.

The Arctic Years

Death was tender last night.
I experienced his warmth
and influence.

He left without me, this morning
but before he went, he said
the arctic years are still to come.
Recollect the freedom
the north will bring to you.

He turned porridge with a wooden spoon,
fed it to me, while I dried snow
from my blue skin with his rough robe,
and watched the candle he had made
from bear fat burn.

I witnessed true dark last night.
The shadows didn't startle me,
but I couldn't move forward into them.

Your dust is not ready
to settle yet. It's not the time
for blood on your breath.

Death held my hands and said
the dead will always be waiting.
Explore the shadows of the forests first,
the darkness of the tundra in winter.

The past is rotten. Leave it outside
the arctic circle. Leave it behind

Work from within. Look forward
to spring from a distance, where
you can quickly drift into the great,
white expanse of the north.

Polar Bear Highway

I can feel the weight of his walk.
It rumbles through my spine like
a volcano preparing to erupt.

I close my eyes so tight they
ache, and my head is filled
with white noise and pain.

I quietly pray to a God I didn't
give a shit about until now.

I am no longer warm in my
goose down sleeping back.
I am coated in cold sweat.

He is down on all fours.
He can smell me, he can taste
the fear I am soaking in.

I ask God for a darker night.
I don't want to see my death in detail.

His claws penetrate the fabric
wall, slashing them open.

I didn't want to ever get this close.
We are eye to eye when he opens
his mouth. His gums are black,
teeth yellow as creamed corn.

He lifts me from my sleeping bag
as easily as a mother scoops up
her newborn.

His teeth clamp over my head.
I am dragged across grass, across shale.
His teeth will soon meet the warm
softness of my brain, and it will all be over.

I will die just 530 miles from the Arctic Circle.

From my limited viewpoint, I can see
snatches of new green growth where
there ought to be thick ice and dense snow.

Flares and gun shots fill the sky like
the stars have declared war with the moon.

I am released unwillingly, my entire body
crunches and cracks on connection
with stones tumbled smooth in the fjord.

The polar bear moves away still hungry.
My head is sticky, wet and fragile,
like the day I first met the world.

Katie Metcalfe

Powerful Echo

The night you decided not to come back
from sleep, I knew. I didn't close my eyes.
Instead, I remembered all you had taught me.

To turn the polar bear's head to the sun,
so he can find his way home.

How to keep my chin and cheeks
from getting blackened by cold.

How to find the base of my grief,
manage it with company of friends,
my dogs and narwhal meat.

You had a smile for death. I heard
no gasp of sadness, no struggle,
no unwillingness to let go.

You went as quietly as a seal
from its breathing hole.

You taught me that to make a tattoo
I would need a bone needle, thread
blackened in the soot of a stone oil lamp.

You taught me that during pregnancy,
a woman should not eat caribou tongue,
marrow or innards, nor the front paws of an animal.

When I was a child, you recollected how
my mother sliced through my umbilical cord
with a slither of ice, then licked me clean.
How I cried out, demanding a name.

You swallowed worlds, regurgitated them
as stories, when the sea froze, the days
started to get dark and another kind of cold.

It has been almost a year since I took
the white man's liquorice
out from your pockets
and shared it with the children.

Almost a year since we dressed you
in your most beautiful winter garments,
carefully placed stones across your body.

I have come to you, nearly every day,
to talk, softly, about the people, our village.

My wife's belly is tight with child.
I put my head close, and can hear
the powerful echo as he turns.
He will have your name.

Poor Hunting Grounds

As a child, I was forced out
of my skins, and into buttoned
shirts and trousers.

They cut my hair, soaped
my neck, ears and face. The bad
tasting block irritated my skin
more than the cold.

Today, I watch my grandson eat
crisps out of foil packets that make
enough noise to scare away all the seals.

I was pushed into the only school
for Eskimos, where teachers spoke
a language I'd never heard.

'Embrace a white lifestyle,' they told us.
'It's time to stop being savages.'

But I returned to the ice. Refused
their language, forgot the dates
they told me I must memorise.

Now, I hold my culture tightly,
with both hands, while those
around me run their fingers
down across their spines and smile
because of their skinniness.

I worry about my grandson,
a young man unable to recognise
the shape of a beluga whale.

He drifts and flickers, a stuttering fire.
He doesn't care how another bear

was found, neck stretched as if
it was determined to march on after death.

He stares at his electronic accessories,
waiting impatiently for the recharge button
to change from red to green.

He doesn't know what to do
with his fingers, and touches
an empty beer bottle.

He gets angry about the silence.

He won't remember the sun
coming through the roof of the igloo
or the day his little brother was born.

He has a fit when a cent goes missing.
Shadows collect in his face.

Before, the Inuit would die by freezing
or starvation. Today it is alcoholism or suicide.

I say this aloud, but he holds up a hand,
mood on fire. He's replying to an email
while I soften leather with my teeth.

Winter Loss

The wolves have fractured
the ice walls of our food cache.

The floor, devoid of flesh,
is deeply scuffed with prints.

The animals danced to a
wild song, before retreating,
back through the broken walls
jaws heavy with flesh.

New prints lead out across
the ice and disappear.

The air smells of wet fur,
defrosted blubber and shit.
The dogs grow quiet.

I fold up my hunger and heartbreak,
place both deep in the pockets
of my polar bear pants.

We wait for the caribou,
but they have already passed.

No fish take our bait. The rabbits
have become better at hiding.

The dogs grow scrawny and miserable,
their courage left behind with the prints
of the wolves. They shake as the wind
rattles through their bones.

My girls, once chubby and happy,
now have the space of a triangle
between their thighs.

We take the dogs down one by one.
The rich history that once rolled
in their eyes has long since left.

They take the bullets with courage.
I see their spirits leave to catch
up with the wolves.

I tell my girls to look, to watch the spirits.
They peer out over the ice, fists clenched in
anticipation.

The dog meat lasts days, not weeks.
The clothes from our backs come next
my girls cry as I tell them to use
their hair to keep warm.

I am dividing our last piece of cloth,
my girls are asleep, tangled in
each other's hair. My husband says
'when I die, eat me. I will taste of caribou.'

There is much love in his dying days,
and when the warmth fades from his eyes,
we wash his body with snow and kisses.

The knife is still sharp and we eat chunks
of his flesh before his lips have even
taken a bluish edge.

The girls go next. They die together.
I eat their flesh in small pieces in
between screams.

Winter passes slowly.
Most days I kneel on a last
piece of caribou skin and stay silent.

The isolation makes me
more aware of everything.

It is spring when my igloo starts melting,
when I see familiar faces from the village
through the translucent walls.

'I am not human anymore,' I say as they
help me into a sealskin parka.
'I have eaten others.'

They speak softly, kind words
that begin the thawing of my heart,
while leading me to open water and home.

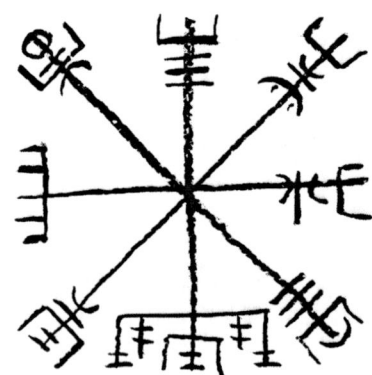

While Out Collecting Birch Sap

The dog points his snout and takes in
the air, jerking his tapered head.

He starts to growl, a low, feral sound
that makes my friend whisper, 'we must
always remember he was once a wolf.'

I continue plugging the birch tree from which
I have just extracted a Coke bottle of sap.
I stroke it, like the back of a relative
after a long sickness.

We will make syrup, and tomorrow,
eat it with elderflower fritters
and wine saved from winter.

The dog begins to recite a mournful
song, which travels around the trees
and comes back to meet us.

When I see the bear crush his sweet skull,
I start to choke on the tragedy and move
at the same time.

But the bear is fast.

I watch my friend make for the horizon,
while my body is overtaken and I meet
the ground face on.

His claws peel back my scalp from where
my frown lines start, to the birthmark
on the back of my neck.

The pain as my skull is exposed
to the forest floor turns my body
rigid as the birch trunk I was draining.

He thinks I am dead. I can smell
my blood on his hot, sour breath.

He smothers me with forest debris,
claws raking the earth to drag it up.
I am left to be devoured later.

The pain grows like a fire in a wood
shed midsummer.

There is soil between my teeth,
clogging up my nose. Stuffed under
my eyelids. I prepare myself to die.

When the gun goes off, the forest
falls still.

The ground around me is damp
with bodily fluids. The smell of shit
and piss and blood is suffocating.

When help comes, they press bandages
around my scalp and swallow repeatedly.

One vomits blueberries and shame.

I ask them if the bear is dead.
They tell me yes.

I ask them where my dog is.
They point to his carcass.

I ask them for my friend.
They nod towards the bear.

She is skinning him quickly, hands steady.
Her face is wax pale and set.

At the bear's mouth, blood blossoms,
and his unfurled paws face upwards
towards the sun.

Katie Metcalfe

Whistling At The Lights

I know that in winter
seal is better than caribou.

I can wait longer at a seal hole
than any other man in the village,
but your father still laughs at my igloos,
and refuses me your hand.

I know to cut blocks from a
wind packed snowdrift.
To curve them upwards
and fit them closely together.

But there is never enough speed
in my fingers, to finish before
the others, before shadows
swallow the sun.

I know not to whistle at the lights,
as they'd come down and cut off my head.

I watch you sewing your amauti *
with your bone needle and sinew thread,
with the compartment for a small child
at the back, below the hood.

In your belly, a child that is not mine
circles, and the pain is worse
than when I helped my grandfather
turn his clothes inside out.

I build my igloo slowly,
smoothing each block with care,
as if nursing a friend back to health
after a bear attack.

Daylight seeps through the ceiling,
and I think of when language
with you was impossible,
because I loved you so much.

I think of the hard times I carved
into a knife handle.

I wanted to last a lifetime with you,
but my life was minus life.

Seeing your belly bloom
under your skins, unfolded
the thread of old and new hurt.

I think of the day I turned violent
against the man of your child,
because I wanted the good taste
of your name in my mouth always.
But when you turned to scream at me
you were still so beautiful.

I imagine if my hands would
have been quicker, and your father
had let me have you.

I imagine searching your body like
my eyes would search broad oceans.

I turn my clothes inside out,
hear gulls overhead, and when
the lights flicker, I whistle.

The amauti is a parka worn by Inuit women.

The Passing Of The Longest Night

The thick scent of bear
drives under the cabin door.
I put my head against the cold
floorboards. I can hear him move.

The dog is barking. Father tells
me to wrap up warm, be ready.

There is shit stuffed deep between
the groves of my boots from this
morning, when we collected snow
shoe hares from their traps.

Mine was the only one still alive.
Father showed me where to place
my hands, where to apply pressure.

He never said don't look into its eyes,
so I did. It stung as bad as a nettle lightly
touching the thin skin of an ankle.

I fondled its pelt, pale as my shoulders
on the first day of summer.

Father told me to hang it around
my neck and hurry up.

He said the muck on my boots
was bear shit.

He said that the soft, dense smelling
dirt had fallen from the backside
of a big male, getting ready to
retreat under earth.

Getting ready to sleep and wait for
spring, when hunters rest their guns,
and iced beads at the tips of tree limbs melt.

After the last dog had his belly ripped
open and eaten, I asked if we could bring
in the new one. I got a clip on the ear.

The bear moves away. He is heavy,
stocked with sacred fuel.

After the first gunshot, I move outdoors.
I can't see my father on his eerie harvest,
but this bear is a screamer.

I wonder if he was the runt
of a cluster of cubs.

The forest night kisses Father's bullets,
but it don't bless them. They land deep
in tree trunks and are silenced.

I can smell his gun and know exactly
when he makes the killing shot.
The silence is tight. Nothing moves.

The morning after and the bear
wears a crown of frost.

There are bloody frozen prints,
tufts of fur missing from his
enormous shoulders.

There will be plenty
of warm nests this winter.

I lean on his joints until they crack apart.
Cold air sets in my mouth as I move

around the body of this giant berserker.
My father says we have to move
quickly. He reminds me that
at certain points of decay,
a bear's forearms and paws
resemble that of a human.

There is no real celebration in my heart,
as father pulls back the skin, revealing
solid, cold flesh marbled with clean white fat.

I feel guilty for having feelings,
for not keeping my hunter instincts close.

The cabin is warm with sleep, but there
is the presence of everything dead.

I imagine ghostly armies of bears
moving soundlessly through the trees.

This evening we ate good meat, intense
with flavour. We ate both eyeballs,
the brain and tongue.

I wish I had chance to smell him
properly before the end, while his breath
still made clouds around his wet snout.

I wish I had pushed my face
into his dense fur, and breathed
everything from his life into my lungs.

I would have told him that real freedom
is on the other side of this sorry place.

I taste my forbidden sadness,
try to swallow it whole and fail.

About the Author

Katie Metcalfe is an English writer, poet and blogger with a 1st Class BA (Hons) in Creative Writing. She has been widely published in print and online. Her poetry collections include, *One of Many Knots, The Absence of Trees and The Long Stillness*. She is the founder of *Wyrd Words & Effigies* blog and magazine. Much of her writing is influenced by Scandinavian culture, history and landscapes. Currently, she is working on a guide to contemporary dark northern culture, as well as a book examining Norwegian identity. More information can be found at her website: katiemariemetcalfe.weebly.com

NORDLAND PUBLISHING

Follow the North Road.

nordlandpublishing.com
facebook.com/nordlandpublishing
nordlandpublishing.tumblr.com

NORDLAND

www.nordlandpublishing.com

CPSIA information can be obtained
at www.ICGtesting.com
Printed in the USA
LVOW07s1944300717

543176LV00001B/33/P